Carl J. Haak

Studies in MALACHI

Second Edition

REFORMED
FREE PUBLISHING
ASSOCIATION

Jenison, Michigan

Scripture cited is taken from the Authorized (King James) Version

Second edition 2014

Reformed Free Publishing Association
1894 Georgetown Center Drive
Jenison MI 49428
www.rfpa.org
mail@rfpa.org

Book design and typesetting by Erika Kiel

ISBN 978-1-936054-50-3
LCCN 2014950481

Foreword

Something that increases our understanding of God's word is to be highly valued. Hence *Studies in Malachi* is to be highly valued.

Thanks to Pastor Haak for bringing to our attention a book of the Bible that is not often studied. However, this last book of the Old Testament is very much worth our study, for he shows that it was written in a time that corresponds to the present day. The chief exhortation of the prophecy of Malachi is most appropriate for our day, namely, that the worship of the Lord be sincere. Always present is the danger that the worship of God becomes a habit. This danger lies especially with ministers and teachers (the priests of today), and they received Malachi's special attention.

Pastor Haak tells us that Malachi's cure for improper worship was an eager anticipation for the fulfillment of God's promise to send his Son. As God used John the Baptist to prepare the way of the Lord Jesus Christ by the preaching of repentance, may God use our study of Malachi to prepare us for the second coming of the Lord Jesus Christ, who comes as judge as well as savior.

It is to be appreciated that this study booklet is written by one who has not only the title of a pastor, but also the heart of a pastor. It is evident that the author's love for the sheep is an extension of his love for the Chief Shepherd.

Thanks to Rev. Haak for making his work of preaching a series of sermons on the prophecy of Malachi to benefit not only those who heard the sermons, but also now all who use this study guide.

Ronald Van Overloop

Lesson 1

Overview of Malachi

Introduction

The book of Malachi is the last Old Testament prophecy written before the birth of Jesus Christ. Approximately four hundred years of silence would follow the words of this prophecy, until the time Gabriel would be sent to godly Zacharias and Elisabeth to announce the birth of the forerunner of our Lord (Mal. 3:1; 4:5; 6; Luke 1:1–20).

The importance of this book of the Bible cannot be overstated. The times in which Malachi prophesied correspond exactly to our own; the sins current among God's people and the temptations to which they were exposed correspond to our day as well. Therefore the "burden of the word of the LORD to Israel by Malachi" (Mal. 1:1) comes to us with the same urgency as it did to them. Let us pay good heed to the sobering words of this book.

Malachi brings us to the post-captivity period, the time after the remnant of Judah had returned from exile in Babylon. The people had been back in Canaan about one hundred years when God sent Malachi to them. The exact date of Malachi's prophecy cannot be determined. Best estimates place it between Nehemiah's two visits to Jerusalem.

Of the man Malachi we know very little, and nothing is revealed about him in the book itself, other than that his name fittingly means "my messenger." He appears on the scene much the way Elijah did (1 Kings 17:1) and with a very similar message and ministry.

We know more about the times in which Malachi prophesied and the evils that were present. The people had completed the temple, but its worship and priesthood had become corrupt (Mal. 1:6–2:8). A new generation had risen that was characterized by cold formalism and spiritual indifference. They no longer had much hope for the coming of the Messiah (Mal. 3:1–6). There was an unwillingness to part with money and possessions for the kingdom of God (v. 8). Marriages were based on lust and not on the love of God. Ungodly divorce was openly practiced (Mal. 2:10–17). All of it was really nothing less than spiritual insensitivity to the love of God (Mal. 1:2–14).

How applicable to us today! How much of the church of Jesus Christ, regardless now of the denomination, is tempted with the same sickly indifference and spiritual laxity, with the attitude that it does not make any difference if we serve God or not! The burden of Malachi is the burden to us, namely, that we turn to the Lord God in love and true worship and eagerly await the promise of his Son!

In addition to the relevance of Malachi to our day, we will be blessed in the study of this book because Malachi emphasizes the covenant of God and its implications for our lives and calls us to look for the coming of the "Sun of righteousness" (Mal. 4:2).

To place Malachi's prophecy clearly in our minds, we should remember the following main events of the post-captivity period:

606–586 BC	Judah is taken captive and Jerusalem is destroyed (2 Kings 25).
606–536 BC	The seventy years of captivity (Jer. 29:10).
536 BC	Zerubbabel leads fifty thousand Jews back to Judah (2 Chron. 36:22; Ezra 1; Isa. 45:1–4).
535 BC	The rebuilding of the temple is begun, but soon halted (Ezra 4:23–24).
520 BC	Darius orders the temple to be completed. Haggai and Zechariah encourage the people (Hag. 1:1–15; 2:19; Ezra 6:14–15).
516 BC	The temple is completed.

478 BC	Esther becomes queen of Persia.
457 BC	Ezra's journey to Jerusalem (Ezra 7:7–9).
444 BC	Nehemiah is sent to Jerusalem. The walls are rebuilt (Neh. 1–2).

The time of Malachi.

| 432 BC | Nehemiah returns the second time to Judah (Neh. 13:7). |

Study Questions and Activities

1. Begin by reading through the book in one sitting. Write down your first impressions.

2. Read through the prophecy again, this time taking notes on any references to the following:

   a. The *time* Malachi wrote (setting and historical background)

   b. The *people* to whom he wrote

   c. The *basic message* he brought to them

3. Make lists of the evils present in God's people and what God's word says to them about these evils.

Evils   God's word

4. List the prophecies of the birth or coming of Jesus Christ given in this book.

5. Prepare an outline of Malachi, giving the major divisions and what you feel is the unifying theme.

6. Using a Bible dictionary or Bible encyclopedia, do some research on the historical setting of this book.

   a. How many returns from Babylon were there?

   b. Who led them?

   c. What was the purpose for each return?

d. What was life like for the Jews at that time?

e. Who were the Samaritans? Find references to the Samaritans in the Bible.

7. Why should we study the book of Malachi?

8. What should be the goals of a study of the book of Malachi?

"The burden of the word of the Lord to Israel by Malachi. I have loved you, saith the Lord. Yet ye say, wherein hast thou loved us? Was not Esau Jacob's brother? saith the Lord: yet I loved Jacob."—Malachi 1:1–2

"Nevertheless I have somewhat against thee, because thou hast left thy first love. Remember therefore from whence thou art fallen, and repent, and do the first works; or else I will come unto thee quickly, and will remove thy candlestick out of his place, except thou repent." Revelation 2:4–5

Recommended Resources

Bromiley, Geoffrey W., ed. *The International Standard Bible Encyclopedia.*

Calvin, John. *Commentaries on the Twelve Minor Prophets.* Translated by John Owen. Vol. 5. *Zechariah and Malachi.* Grand Rapids, MI: Eerdmans, 1950.

Davies, John D. *A Dictionary of the Bible.*

Henry, Matthew. *Matthew Henry's Commentary on the Whole Bible*. Vol. 4. *Isaiah to Malachi*. McLean, VA: Mac Donald Publishing Company.

Lubbers, George. 1964. "Exposition of the Prophecy of Malachi." *Standard Bearer* 40 (7): 156–57.

———. 1964. "Exposition of the Prophecy of Malachi." *Standard Bearer* 40 (8): 179–180.

———. 1964. "Exposition of the Prophecy of Malachi." *Standard Bearer* 40 (9): 203–4.

———. 1964. "Exposition of the Prophecy of Malachi." *Standard Bearer* 40 (10): 228–29.

———. 1964. "Exposition of the Prophecy of Malachi." *Standard Bearer* 40 (11): 252–53.

———. 1964. "Exposition of the Prophecy of Malachi." *Standard Bearer* 40 (12): 276–77.

———. 1964. "Exposition of the Prophecy of Malachi." *Standard Bearer* 40 (14): 325–26.

———. 1964. "Exposition of the Prophecy of Malachi." *Standard Bearer* 40 (15): 350–51.

———. 1964. "Exposition of the Prophecy of Malachi." *Standard Bearer* 40 (16): 374–75

———. 1964. "Exposition of the Prophecy of Malachi." *Standard Bearer* 40 (18): 422–23.

Moore, T. V. *Haggai and Malachi*. The Geneva Series of Commentaries. Edinburgh: Banner of Truth Trust, 1974.

PRCA [Protestant Reformed Churches in America]. 2005. *The Confessions and the Church Order of the Protestant Reformed Churches*. Grandville, MI: PRCA.

Tenney, Merrill C., ed. *The Zondervan Pictorial Bible Dictionary*. Grand Rapids, MI: Zondervan Publishing House, MI, 1963.

Lesson 2

God's Love Questioned, Proven, and Confessed

Malachi 1:1–5

Introduction

The first five verses of this prophecy deserve serious and concentrated study by every believer. Why?

First, the words "I have loved you" stand as the foundation of the entire book, as well as the ground on which God brings his complaint against his people. All the terrible spiritual indifference, the weariness of worshiping God, the violation of God's covenant in the married state, all of which was prevalent in Malachi's day, was at the heart this: insensitivity and coldness to the love of God. God's first word in this prophecy strikes to the very heart of the problem of the spiritual apathy and carelessness of that day and of our day.

Second, these first five verses reveal the truth of predestination, the heartbeat of the gospel. Sovereign predestination— eternal election and reprobation—is the truth that ascribes all glory in salvation to God, and God alone. God teaches this great truth not as abstract, cold dogma, but specifically as the battering ram against spiritual lukewarmness, and for the purpose of comforting God's people. Indeed, what greater word from God could we possibly hear than "I have loved you, saith the LORD" (Mal. 1:2).

Malachi shows that the people of his day were questioning the reality of God's eternal love to them. Judging from what could be seen, they were sorely tempted to doubt that love. The Samaritans, the people who lived to the north, had been bitterly hostile and had opposed the building of the temple. They accused the Jews of disloyalty to Cyrus. Also, there had been severe crop failures, droughts, and plagues that had consumed the harvests. And the people had become the plaything of the nations. Thus with almost a cynical tone, they asked, "Wherein hast thou loved us?" (Mal. 1:2).

We must look at ourselves, as we too, in the light of sickness, pain, trials, and depression are tempted to ask the same question.

The proof of God's love toward his people is found in the words of God to Rebekah (Gen 25:23). The Holy Spirit in Malachi and later in Paul (Rom. 9:1) shows that these words to Rebekah speak of the truth of eternal, sovereign election and reprobation. Election is God's choosing from all eternity the persons who will be saved. God's choice of them is not based on anything in them, but is only out of his grace and mercy (John 6:39; Rom. 8:29–30; Eph. 1:1–4; 1 Pet. 2:9; Canons of Dordt 1.7, 9–10). Reprobation is God's eternal and just damnation of the persons who will perish, and that in the way of their sins (Matt. 15:13–14; Rom. 9:17–22; 1 Pet. 2:6–8; Canons of Dordt 1.15; Belgic Confession 16).

It is vital to see that Jehovah speaks these truths in the context of *comforting* and *confirming* his people. Further, Jehovah God, in proving his sovereign and unconditional love for his people, refers to the well-known history of Jacob and Esau, the twin brothers born to Isaac and Rebekah (Gen. 25; Rom. 9:10–13). The sovereignty, graciousness, unconditionality, and justice of God's predestination are shown in this biblical example.

We are to confess God's predestinating love! "And ye shall say, The Lord will be magnified" (Mal. 1:5). Cold indifference to the God who has said to us unworthy sinners, "I have loved you"? God shame us if that is ever the case in our hearts. Rather than sickly indifference, we who believe and experience the Reformed and biblical truth of predestination ought to sound forth praises of God for his fathomless and unquenchable love.

Study Questions and Activities

1. The idea of the "burden of the word of the Lord" (v. 1)

    a. What other Old Testament prophets use this terminology?

b. What is the meaning and significance of *"burden* of the...LORD"?

c. How is God's word a burden to us?

2. God's love questioned (v. 2)

   a. What do the following verses teach about God's love?

      1) Deuteronomy 7:7–8

      2) Isaiah 38:17

      3) John 15:19

      4) Romans 5:5–11

      5) Ephesians 1:4–5

      6) 1 John 3:1

      7) 1 John 4:8–10, 19

8) Revelation 3:19

b. Define God's love.

c. In what ways do we question the love of God toward us? Be specific.

d. How ought the knowledge of God's love be our daily comfort?

e. Discuss and prove from scripture this statement: The love of God toward his people is not measured in things or in the absence of things, but solely in the cross of Jesus Christ.

f. Discuss and prove from scripture this statement: God's love toward us may not be questioned.

3. God's love proven

a. How does Paul use Malachi 1:2 in Romans 9:13?

b. Read the articles of the Canons of Dordt mentioned in the introduction (1. 7, 9–10, 15) and the scriptural passages in support of election (John 6:39; Rom. 8:29–30;

Eph. 1:1–4; 1 Pet. 2:9) and reprobation (Matt. 15:13–14; Rom. 9:17–22; 1 Pet. 2:6–8).

c. What is meant by the following?

   1) Unconditional election

   2) Sovereign election

   3) Gracious or free election

   4) Just reprobation

   5) Particular election

d. Why is the example of Jacob and Esau so appropriate in proving God's sovereign predestination?

e. How does God's hatred of Edom (Esau) prove his love for Jacob (his people)?

f. What ought to be our response to these truths (2 Thess. 2:13; 2 Tim. 2:19)?

g. How should these truths produce the following?

   1) Humility

   2) Assurance

   3) Adoration of God

   4) Thankfulness

   5) Zeal for missions and witnessing

h. The boast of the Edomites and the Lord's answer

   1) Who was Edom?

   2) Look up the words *Edom* and *Edomites* in a Bible concordance and give a brief review of Edom and its significance.

   3) What attitude did the Edomites express in verse 4?

      (a) Do we see this attitude today?

(b) Do we even fight this attitude in ourselves?

4) What do we learn in the strong answer of the Lord to Edom's boast?

4. God's love confessed

a. What did God promise that Israel would see (v. 5)?

b. Did God promise anything more than Edom's destruction?

c. What does this promise mean for us today?

d. In what ways ought the confession of God's gracious love toward us be evidenced in our lives and words?

"And not only this; but when Rebecca also had conceived by one, even by our father Isaac; (For the children being not yet born, neither having done any good or evil, that the purpose of God according to election might stand, not of works, but of him that calleth;) It was said unto her, The elder shall serve the younger. As it is written Jacob have I loved, but Esau have I hated."—Romans 9:10–13

Lesson 3

Where is My Honor?

Malachi 1:6–14

Introduction

The loving reverence for God, the sincere worship of his holy name, the living service and dedicated lives that are alone worthy of God, were all absent among the people of Malachi's day. This was evident in the manner in which they worshiped God. It was not that the temple was abandoned and the outward rites of religion altogether neglected, but it was all performed in a cold, indifferent, and resentful way. This was especially true of the priests, the spiritual leaders, but it characterized also the people as a whole.

The basic instruction of this section of the book of Malachi is well summarized by John Calvin in his commentary:

> Nothing is indeed so precious as his worship; and he had instituted under the law sacrifices and other rites, that they might worship him spiritually. The whole of religion is despised when one despises the external acts of worship according to the law.

The corruption of the true worship of God came out in three ways.

First, it was evident in what was offered. The Old Testament law of sacrifices was very clear (Lev. 22:17–33; Deut. 17:1). The people offered "polluted bread" (Mal. 1:7); "the lame and the sick" (v. 8); "that which was torn, and the lame, and sick" (v. 13); a female of the flock when they had a male (v. 14).

Second, the corruption was evident in the awful attitude they had toward the worship of God. The Lord requires a broken and contrite heart (Ps. 50:7–23; 51:17; Hos. 6:6; Micah 6:6–8). Instead they considered the worship of God "weariness" and "snuffed at it" (Mal. 1:13).

Third, corruption was evident in the crass and hardened impenitence they showed when God reproved them for all of this. When God's prophet confronted them with their terrible sins, they had the audacity to deny them (vv. 6–7). That is pride at its worst.

The prophet brought reproof! He told them that Jehovah had, in two respects, a just cause against them. First, "If then I be a father, where is mine honour?" (v. 6). The truth that the almighty God, for the sake of Jesus Christ, is become my Father ought to evoke the deepest honor, respect, reverence, and awe before him, which will be seen in how we worship him and how we live before him. Second, "If I be a master, where is my fear?" (v. 6). Malachi brought out the truth of God's sovereignty when he referred to God as "the LORD of hosts" (vv. 8, 11, 14). Because he is the master of the heavenly hosts and king of all glory, nothing but the deepest, humblest fear and reverential awe ought to characterize the people who worship him and call him their God.

This study ends with God's powerful assertion that he will be worshiped by a people gathered out of all the earth (v. 11; Zech. 8:23; John 4:21–23). This is a beautiful, powerful, and comforting prophecy of the gathering of the church of Jesus Christ in the new dispensation, the existence of which is for the sole purpose of rendering praise and worship to his name. Why is this so certain? "For I am a great King, saith the LORD of hosts" (v. 14).

Does this word of God speak to you? How does it find you in respect to your worshiping God? What about your attendance at the house of God? What about your prayers? your reading of scripture? your entire life as you are to live it in sincere praise of God? Put yourself before the question: "If then I be a father, where is mine honour? and if I be a master, where is my fear?"

Study Questions and Activities

1. True worship of God

a. We must remember that worship is not academic; for God, who is a great king and our sovereign Lord by grace, requires us to worship him. What constitutes true worship of God?

b. What is the meaning of the word *worship*?

c. Consult a Bible dictionary and find verses in scripture that express the idea of worship.

d. What do the following texts teach about worship?

1) Psalm 95:6

2) Psalm 96:9

3) Psalm 81:9

4) Matthew 18:20

5) Revelation 7:9–12

6) Revelation 15:4

e. What is the purpose of worship (Ps. 27:4; 84:1–3; 122:1–4)?

f. What is meant by the following characteristics of true worship?

   1) In spirit and in truth (Ps. 51:15–17; Isa. 1:10–17; 57:15; John 4:24)

   2) Reverence (Ps. 89:7)

   3) Humility (Micah 6:6–8; Hos. 6:6)

   4) Joyful, thankful, and active (Ps. 96:1–2; 111:1)

g. What does the second commandment teach about the true worship of God (Heidelberg Catechism, Lord's Day 35)?

h. Think about and discuss these statements: Worship is not first for us, but for God. The question to be asked of any worship service is not first, what did I get out of it? but did it bring glory to God?

2. The shameful abuse of worship in Malachi's day, the spiritual attitude it revealed, the judgment of God upon it, and the warning it gives to us

a. List the abuses of the worship of God that Malachi exposed.

1) To what does "polluted bread upon mine altar" refer? Does it refer to the table of showbread or to all the sacrifices in general?

2) What were the requirements regarding the animals sacrificed to God (Lev. 22:17–33)?

3) Why were those requirements important (1 Pet. 1:18–20)?

4) What was the priests' responsibility in all of this?

5) What does Malachi mean by "who is there even among you that would shut the doors for nought" (v. 10)?

6) Who is the deceiver in verse 14?

7) What is his deception?

b. What attitudes were present among the priests?

c. Explain these attitudes over against Isaiah 1:10–17.

d. What is meant by the responses of the people in verses 6–7 to the charges against them of their failure to honor and to fear God in their worship?

e. Why are these responses so chilling and dreadful?

3. Jehovah brings out that this irreverence and apathy is an attack on his fatherhood and sovereignty.

a. What does it mean that God is our Father (Matt. 7:7–11; Rom. 8:15–17; Gal. 4:4–7; Heidelberg Catechism, Lord's Days 9, 46)?

b. How should God's fatherhood and sovereignty evoke true honor and reverence for God?

c. What is the meaning of the "LORD of hosts"? Consult a Bible dictionary.

d. Explain from 1 Chronicles 29:11 what is implied in the sovereignty of God.

e. How should God's sovereignty evoke deep reverence and tears of repentance in us?

f. Explain the promise of verse 11 in the light of Psalm 113:3, Zechariah 8:23, and John 4:21–23.

g. Let us now in our hearts answer the questions of Malachi 1:6: "If then I be a father, where is mine honour? and if I be a master, where is my fear?"

4. For further study on the laws of sacrifices, consult the following passages:

a. Sin offering (Lev. 4:1–35; 6:24–30)

b. Guilt offering (Lev. 5:14–6:6)

c. Burnt offering (Lev. 1:3–17; 6:8–13)

d. Grain offering (Lev. 2; 6:14–23)

e. Drink offering (Num. 15:1–10)

f. Peace offering (Lev. 3; 7:11–21)

g. Wave offering (Ex. 29:24–27; Lev. 23; Num. 15)

h. Thank offering (Lev. 7:12–15; 22:29)

i. Freewill offering (Lev. 7:16; 22:18–23)

j. Ordination offering (Ex. 29:19–34; Lev. 8:22–32)

"A son honoureth his father, and a servant his master: if then I be a father, where is mine honour? and if I be a master, where is my fear? saith the Lord of hosts unto you, O priests, that despise my name. And ye say, Wherein have we despised thy name? For from the rising of the sun even unto the going down of the same my name shall be great among the Gentiles; and in every place incense shall be offered unto my name, and a pure offering: for my name shall be great among the heathen, saith the Lord of hosts."—Malachi 1:6, 11

The Prayer John Calvin Offered after Expounding on Malachi 1:6–14

Grant, Almighty God, that as thou hast been pleased in thy infinite mercy not only to choose from among us to be priests unto thee, but also to consecrate us all to thyself in thine only begotten Son,— O grant, that we on this day may purely and sincerely serve thee, and so strive to devote ourselves wholly to thee, that we may be pure and chaste in mind, soul, and body, and that thy name so shine forth in all our performances, that thy worship among us may be holy, and pure, and approved by thee, until we shall at length enjoy that glory to which thou invitest us by thy gospel, and which has been obtained for us by the blood of thine only-begotten Son. Amen.

Lesson 4

God's Covenant of Life and Peace

Malachi 2:1–10

Introduction

Malachi's method of exposing the sins of his day is to hold those sins up before the light of God's gracious goodness to his people, thus exposing the horribleness of their sins as they are seen against that background. Later in the prophecy he gives a list of the sordid sins being committed (Mal. 3:5). Here, however, he expresses the depth of those sins, not by going into all the details, but by holding them up before the light of the righteousness and goodness of God. This is proper, for sin's horror is not measured by how many people it harms or how far-reaching the consequences might be. Rather, you and I must know the ugliness of sin by seeing it against the background of God's holiness and goodness.

Malachi advances step by step in exposing the sins of the people. His first word, you remember, was "I have loved you" (Mal. 1:2). How awful is spiritual apathy when revealed against the background of God's sovereign love! Malachi continues by holding up the fatherhood and majesty of God over against the cold, formalistic worship of that day (vv. 6–7).

In chapter 2 Malachi reveals more of God's goodness and holiness: "my covenant was with him of life and peace" (v. 5). The darkness of the sin of Malachi's day was exactly that the people, and especially the priests, corrupted the covenant of God, departed out of its way, and caused many to forsake it.

It will be important for us to understand the truth of the covenant as well as the covenantal calling set before us in this passage. Briefly the passage points out four truths on the covenant.

First, the covenant is a living bond of fellowship between God and us in which we walk with God in peace and equity, and God grants us life and peace. The word *covenant* means "bond" or "union" and implies the most intimate love and fellowship.

Second, the covenant is established (made) by God. This is because it is his covenant: "my covenant was with him." Also, the part of the covenant which is ours, namely to walk with God, is something that God *gives* to us by his grace (v. 5).

Third, there is one covenant of God. God speaks of the covenant with Levi (v. 6). Romans 9, Galatians 3, and other passages teach that there is one covenant of God in all ages, even as there is one God. The covenant with Levi refers especially to Numbers 25:12–13 and emphasizes that all the elect, as members of the covenant, are Levites and priests, that is, dedicated to God and zealous for his glory.

Fourth, we have a calling in the covenant, namely, to reverence our God, walk with our God, and teach others the ways of God.

In Malachi's day the covenant was being corrupted in the most horrible ways. First, Malachi singles out the priests who, rather than being shining examples of dedication and zeal for God, were guilty of dead formalism in their worship (v. 2), and guilty of injustice in administering the law (v. 9). Second, the entire people profaned the covenant in dealing treacherously with their brothers (v. 10; Mal. 3:5). Notice carefully, when God's people are characterized by injustice or deceit in their dealings with one another, God's covenant is profaned. For the covenant deals not only with our relationships to God, but also with our relationships together as the friends of God.

Jehovah always takes his covenant seriously. Nothing is dearer to his heart. The warnings given are severe and frightening (Mal. 2:2–3, 9).

Now we must examine ourselves in the light of these words: "my covenant was with him of life and peace." How do our daily lives measure up to the gracious calling to be dedicated and zealous for Jehovah, our sovereign friend and savior? How do our lives with one another as members of the covenant stand before this truth? May the study of the passage increase in us reverence for God's covenant, a closer walk with God, and a faithful life with one another as members of his covenant.

Study Questions and Activities

1. The profaning of the covenant is the main charge laid against the people (vv. 11–17). Only when we understand the covenant can we see not only the horribleness of corrupting the covenant, but also the blessedness of the covenant for our daily lives.

   a. What is meant by "my covenant was with him of life and peace"?

   b. Read Genesis 15; Jeremiah 31:31–40; 32:36–44; and Hebrews 8:8–3.

   c. Answer the following questions regarding the covenant:

      1) What is God's covenant?

      2) How were covenants made (Gen. 15:9–17; Jer. 34:18)?

      3) What significance is found in the manner covenants were made?

      4) How is God's covenant made with us?

      5) What is emphasized when Malachi adds that the covenant is one *of life and peace*?

d. Malachi points out the calling we have in the covenant of God (vv. 5–8). Show from the passage the following three elements of our calling and explain them:

1) Reverence for God

2) Walking with God

3) Instructing others in the ways of God

e. Malachi speaks of the "covenant of Levi."

1) What is the "covenant of Levi" (Num. 25:12–13)?

2) How many covenants of God are there (Gen. 17:7; Rom. 4:11, 16; Gal. 3:9, 16, 29)?

3) What does the "covenant of Levi" emphasize concerning our calling in God's covenant (1 Pet. 2:9; Rev. 1:6)?

2. The priests corrupted the covenant.

a. List the ways in which the priests profaned God's covenant.

b. What should the priests have done as members of God's covenant?

   1) Apply this to our calling as priests of God.

   2) What does this say to officebearers in the church?

   3) What does this say to officebearers in the home?

3. The people dealt treacherously with God's covenant by false dealings with their brothers (v. 10).

   a. Explain the force of the questions of verse 10: "Have we not all one father? hath not one God created us? why do we deal treacherously every man against his brother, by profaning the covenant of our fathers?"

   b. How does the truth of the covenant bear on our dealings with one another as fellow members of the covenant? Be as specific as you can, mentioning different areas of our lives with one another that bear the stamp of God's covenant.

4. Jehovah warns against corrupting his covenant.

   a. What warnings does he give?

b. What do those warnings mean?

5. Explain what it means to lay these things to our hearts and to give glory to God's name (v. 2).

"My covenant was with him of life and peace; and I gave them to him for the fear wherewith he feared me, and was afraid before my name. The law of truth was in his mouth, and iniquity was not found in his lips: he walked with me in peace and equity, and did turn many away from iniquity. For the priest's lips should keep knowledge, and they should seek the law at his mouth: for he is the messenger of the Lord of hosts. But ye are departed out of the way; ye have caused many to stumble at the law; ye have corrupted the covenant of Levi, saith the Lord of hosts."—Malachi 2:5–8.

Judah's Treachery against the Marriage Bond

Malachi 2:11–17

Introduction

In the first part of chapter 2, Malachi beautifully describes God's covenant, the bond of friendship he made with us in Christ. Malachi shows that the covenant is eternal and was established by Jehovah out of pure grace. In the covenant God blesses his people with life and peace. Those in the covenant have the calling to walk with God, turn from iniquity, oppose evil, and love God's truth.

Against this background the sins of the people of Malachi's day stood out in all their naked ugliness. Their religious attitude was cold and indifferent. A corrupt priesthood failed to teach God's law. The people dealt fraudulently with their brothers.

Now we learn that their sin against the covenant of God was especially in the evil practice of mixed marriages and divorce and remarriage. This is the burden of the word of the Lord in verses 11–16.

The sinful abuses of marriage were twofold.

First, the young men of Judah had profaned the covenant of God by marrying the daughters "of a strange god" (vv. 11–12). This was not new to Malachi's day. From the days of Abraham, Isaac, and Jacob, the sons of God had been warned against this and exhorted to marry in the Lord (Gen. 24:1–9; 26:34–35; 28:2). It was especially this sin that led to Israel's problems and to a generation that knew not the Lord or his mighty acts (Ex. 34:15–16; Deut. 7:3–4; 1 Kings 11:1–13). Israel had committed this sin as late as the days of Ezra and Nehemiah. No sooner had God brought Judah back from captivity in Babylon than the men of Judah began to marry heathen wives (Ezra 9:1–12; Neh. 10:30; 13:26–27). Some sixty years after Ezra in Malachi's day, the men of Judah were again looking for their wives outside the boundaries of Israel. They contracted mixed marriages, spiritually mixed. They built their marriages on the sand and mire of carnal lust and set aside the rock of spiritual oneness in the promise of Christ (Matt. 7:24–27).

Second, the sins against marriage were not confined to the youth, for the married men violated the sacred bond of marriage in divorce. Literally, verse 13 reads, "And a second thing ye do." That second thing was the sinful practice of "putting away [divorcing]" the wives of their youth (vv. 15–16). The men of Judah grew tired of their wives. The weaknesses and problems that every marriage encounters were not overcome with God's word. Rather they let their personal desires and the difficulties of marriage overrule the word of God.

We should ask the question, why does Malachi zero in on this evil rather than on some other? There were certainly other gross violations of God's law present (Mal. 3:5). Why does he concern himself with the sinful abuses of the marriage bond? The answer is that marriage is a picture of Jehovah's covenant. It mirrors God's intimate bond between himself and his people (Hos. 2:19–20; Eph. 5:21–33). By establishing mixed marriages and being unfaithful in marriage, the people had profaned the covenant of God. Because of what marriage is, they had profaned the covenant of God. Because of what marriage is, God requires holiness of his people in the marriage bond. This he loves. All profaning of marriage he hates (Mal. 2:16).

Jehovah looked upon these abuses as treachery (vv. 11, 15–16). Treachery is being false to the one you confess to love, and secretly working to destroy him. Judah's treachery was saying, "I am God's friend" (note verse 12 mentions that they still offered to the Lord), and yet making a mockery of that confession in the way they married and lived in marriage. You could not see devotion to God in the way they selected their wives or in the way they lived with their wives. It was "an abomination" to the Lord, something he hated. God would "cut off the man that doeth this" (v. 12).

How urgent this word of God becomes to us today! In this passage God shows how sacred the bond of marriage is, how pleasing it is to him, and how he hates and punishes all violations of the marriage vow. God will uphold marriage. He will aid and support married persons, even when they are the least deserving, because it is an institution pleasing to him (Form for the Confirmation of Marriage before the Church, in *Confessions and Church Order*, 306–10).

"Take heed to your spirit, that ye deal not treacherously" (v. 16). Love the sacred bond of marriage! This means that we will *daily* desire to be clean before God in all we do in marriage. We must remember that the Lord stands as "witness" over our marriages (v. 14). Then, rather than establishing our marriages carnally and living in marriage selfishly, we will live consciously for his approval and glory.

Verse 17 stands somewhat in isolation from verses 11–16. It is another complaint of Jehovah against his people. This time it is directed against their attitudes. The Jews thought that Jehovah favored the wicked because he did not punish them. They accused God of injustice (compare Ps. 73). Most likely this stemmed from their experiencing severe economic hardships and the lack of national prominence.

Study Questions and Activities

1. We must remember what marriage is and how it is a picture of God's covenant with his people. Only then can we see the treachery of mixed marriages and divorce and remarriage. Only then can we see how we must live in our marriages.

    a. Look up the following texts. What does each one say about what marriage *is?*

    1) Genesis 2:24 (1 Cor. 6:16)

    2) Proverbs 18:22

3) Ephesians 5:32

4) 1 Corinthians 11:11–12

5) 1 Timothy 4:1, 3

b. How is marriage a picture of God's covenant with his people (Hos. 2:19–20; Eph. 5:21–23)?

c. How are the following elements necessary for marriage if it is to picture the covenant of God?

   1) Spiritual oneness

   2) Faithfulness

   3) Forgiveness

   4) Companionship (friendship and communication)

d. Find texts to support your answers above regarding the following elements:

   1) Spiritual oneness

2) Faithfulness

3) Forgiveness

4) Companionship (friendship and communication)

2. The treachery of mixed marriage

   a. Look up the following passages to determine whom a child of God is to marry:

     1) Genesis 24:1–9

     2) Genesis 26:34–35

     3) Genesis 28:2

     4) Exodus 34:16

     5) Deuteronomy 7:3–4

     6) 1 Corinthians 7:39

7) 2 Corinthians 6:14

b. What is the importance of the restrictions regarding marriage?

c. Why is spiritual oneness a necessity for marriage (1 Pet. 3:7)?

d. What does "the LORD will cut off the man that doeth this" mean (v. 12)?

e. How can we teach our children the necessity of establishing solid Christian marriages?

3. The treachery of putting away the "wife of thy youth"

a. What is meant by the following expressions in verse 14 that describe marriage? Apply them to marriage.

1) "Wife of thy youth"

2) "Thy companion"

3) "The wife of thy covenant" (Prov. 2:17)

b. Explain what verse 15 means and tell how it is a powerful argument against "putting away." (God refers to Genesis 2:18–24 and his creation of *one* woman for the man, even though he could conceivably have made more. "Yet had he the residue of the spirit.")

c. Look up the following passages and take brief notes on what they teach regarding God's hatred of "putting away."

1) Matthew 5:33

2) Matthew 19:3–12

3) Mark 10:3–12

4) Luke 16:18

5) 1 Corinthians 7:29

6) Romans 7:2–4

7) Deuteronomy 24:1–4

d. Answer from these verses the following questions:

    1) Is divorce ever permissible?

    2) Is remarriage ever allowable while one's first spouse is living?

    3) Why is it important to maintain that marriage is a lifelong bond that can be broken *only* by death?

e. The women who were wrongly divorced brought their anguish to the Lord (v. 13).

    1) Explain verse 13.

    2) Compare verse 13 with 1 Peter 3:7.

    3) Explain how our spiritual life and health are tied to our marriages.

4. Explain what verse 17 means.

5. Compare verse 17 with Psalm 73 and express how we often give this same complaint and thus weary the Lord.

"And I will betroth thee unto me forever; yea, I will betroth thee unto me in righteousness, and in judgment, and in lovingkindness, and in mercies. I will even betroth thee unto me in faithfulness; and thou shalt know the LORD."—Hosea 2:19–20

Lesson 6

The Coming of the Messenger of the Covenant

Malachi 3:1–6

Introduction

In these verses of the prophecy, Malachi speaks words of consolation and joy to true believers and words of severe judgment and warning to those who walk in wickedness. We have noted that the days in which Malachi prophesied were times of trouble for God's people who had returned from the Babylonian captivity. It was a time of apostasy, cold indifference, and treachery. Even on the part of God's true people there was despondency and secret despair. "Where is the God of judgment?" they ask in Malachi 2:17. A class of rich had arisen whose wealth was gained from their oppression of the poor. For the true believer it was a dark day, a day in which wickedness seemed triumphant.

In answer comes the mighty promise of God's sure judgment on the wicked and his salvation of the righteous. "Behold...the Lord, whom ye seek, shall suddenly come to his temple, even the messenger of the covenant, whom ye delight in." Unto the wicked he will appear as a fire to consume and to execute swift judgment against all who practice wickedness and fear not God. For those who seek and delight him, he will come to purify them and to present them before God in righteousness. And this is certain, for it is the word of the Lord, the one who changes not. Therefore the sons of Jacob, the elect of God, will be preserved even in the darkest of times.

Malachi very plainly speaks of the coming of Jesus Christ. This passage in part is very similar to Isaiah 40:3. Isaiah's prophecy must have been well-known to the Old Testament believers. Malachi refers then to the promise of John the

Baptist, the forerunner (Matt. 3:3; 11:10; Mark 1:3; Luke 1:76; 3:4–6; John 1:23).

Concerning the coming of the promised Savior, the hope and salvation of all the church, Malachi has much to teach us.

First, the coming of the promised Savior will be preceded by "my messenger," whose work would be to prepare the way before him.

Second, the promised Messiah is the "messenger of the covenant," who is the delight as well as the object of faith of all God's people.

Third, the promised Christ is God, equal to and the same as God, one being with Jehovah. Note verse 1: "I will send my messenger...and the Lord, whom ye seek...saith the LORD of hosts."

Fourth, the coming of Christ in both his birth and return in judgment is viewed as one coming. Clearly Malachi speaks of his advent as well as his second coming in judgment.

Fifth, this coming serves a dual purpose. He appears as a flame of fire to take vengeance on the wicked (v. 5). And he comes to purify by fire the sons of Levi that they may offer to God sacrifices of righteousness (v. 3).

Sixth, the passage teaches the certain preservation of the true children of God (v. 6). The perseverance of the saints is guaranteed, not by their unchangeable love to God, but by his unchangeable love to them, and by his eternal purpose and promise in Christ Jesus.

Study Questions and Activities

1. Verse 1 is a beautiful prophecy of the coming and identity of Jesus Christ. Examine it carefully to see its power and beauty.

   a. Show from the New Testament that the messenger who will prepare the way for Christ is John the Baptist.

1) What does it mean that John was to "prepare the way before me"?

2) Is there any correlation to today as we await the final return of Christ?

3) How did John prepare the way for Christ?

4) Why was this preparation necessary?

b. The identity of the promised Messiah

   1) Show from verse 1 that Jesus Christ is God.

   2) Compare this with Romans 9:5 and 1 Timothy 3:16.

   3) Look up Jeremiah 31:31, Hebrews 9:15, and 12:24 and explain what it means that Christ is the messenger of the *covenant*.

   4) What is the relationship between Christ and the covenant?

c. What do the following verses teach concerning the identity of the "temple" in verse 1?

1) Ephesians 2:20–22

2) Zechariah 6:12–15

3) 2 Corinthians 6:16

4) 2 Thessalonians 2:4

5) Jeremiah 7:4

6) Revelation 3:12

d. What does it mean that Christ "shall suddenly come to his temple"?

2. The purpose of Christ's coming is judgment and salvation.

a. What is the significance of Malachi's seeing the advent of Christ in Bethlehem and his final return as one coming?

b. What do the following passages teach concerning what the coming of Christ is to the wicked and unbeliever?

   1) 2 Thessalonians 1:7–10

   2) Revelation 6:13–17

   3) Luke 2:34

c. Christ comes to "purify" and to "purge" the sons of Levi (v. 3).

   1) Explain how the purifying of silver by fire is an example of Christ's work in believers (Prov. 17:3; 1 Pet. 1:7).

   2) Who are the "sons of Levi"?

   3) Compare Malachi 3:4 with 1 Peter 2:9 and Ephesians 5:26–27.

   4) What is the meaning of Malachi 3:4?

d. Make a list of the sins mentioned in verse 5.

e. Find other scriptures that mention the evils in verse 5 and that describe what the sins are.

f. How are all of these sins summed under "and fear not me" (v. 5)?

3. The preservation of saints is founded on the being of God.

   a. What do the following passages say about God's immutability (unchangeableness)?

      1) Psalm 102:26–27 (quoted in Heb. 1:11–12)

      2) James 1:17

      3) Numbers 23:19

      4) 2 Timothy 2:13

   b. What is God's immutability?

   c. What is the reason for the preservation of the saints?

d. Why does the preservation of the saints produce comfort and carefulness in the saints and not fear, or discomfort, and carelessness?

"Behold, I will send my messenger, and he shall prepare the way before me: and the Lord, whom ye seek, shall suddenly come to his temple, even the messenger of the covenant, whom ye delight in: behold, he shall come, saith the Lord of hosts. But who may abide the day of his coming? and who shall stand when he appeareth? for he is like a refiner's fire, and like fuller's soap: And he shall sit as a refiner and purifier of silver: and he shall purify the sons of Levi, and purge them as gold and silver, that they may offer unto the Lord an offering in righteousness. For I am the Lord, I change not; therefore ye sons of Jacob are not consumed." Malachi 3:1–3, 6

Lesson 7

Will a Man Rob God?

Malachi 3:7–12

Introduction

We see repeatedly in the study of Malachi how the prophet's day and our own are so much alike. The sins present among God's people then are similar to those today, especially the merely outward observance of religion and the cold, formal worship of the true God. We have also observed how Malachi deals with these sins, namely, by always holding them up to the light (brightness) of God in order to show how heinous and treacherous it is when people sin against the goodness and mercy of the Lord, depart from his ordinances, and render him the service of a carnal heart.

We have seen another penetrating, applicable, and urgent lesson in these verses. It deals with the "worship of giving" (2 Cor. 8–9). It is the call to supply the needs of God's church and kingdom, as well as to show benevolence to the poor.

The evil exposed in Malachi 3:7–12 is the failure to bring the tithes and offerings to God's house (v. 8). These "ordinances" (v. 7) were clearly marked out in the Old Testament scriptures. It was a common sin of the covenant people, one which their fathers had committed and for which they had been punished. Now the restored exiles from Babylon settled (fallen) into the same sin. Evidently the Lord had chastened them with "a curse" (v. 9), "the devourer," and that which "destroys the fruit of the ground" (v. 11). A famine, pestilence, or plagues of some sort had been sent (Joel 1:4). Yet the people, in the hardness of their hearts, did not see this as the word of God's rebuke, but hoarded for themselves whatever was left.

The heinousness of this sin and the underlying rebellion, distrust, and covetousness are exposed by the "messenger" of God.

First, this sin was hereditary (Mal. 3:7). History seems to have taught them nothing, although their history was full of examples of the Lord's faithful and gracious care and his heavy chastisements upon their fathers' covetousness and greed. (Ps. 78; Dan. 9:3–19; Ezek. 9; Acts 7).

Second, the people "robbed" God by their sin (v. 8). The question is biting and arresting: "will a man rob God?" The principle of the eighth commandment is at work. It reveals that in stealing and in failing to serve the Lord with the possessions entrusted to us, we are insolent and incredibly defiant (Heidelberg Catechism, Lord's Day 42).

Third, the people were hardened in this sin, and their stinginess revealed their spiritual bareness. To God's call "Return unto me!" (Mal 3:7), they respond, "Wherein shall we return?" That is, they were so ignorant of themselves and of the spiritual demands of God's law, that they could see nothing in themselves for which they should repent, and rather saw themselves justified in the way they dealt with their possessions. More: to Jehovah's reproof, "Ye have robbed me" (v. 8), they have the audacity to say, "Wherein?" That is, they refused (as we do so often) to own up to their sin of coveting and of hoarding for ourselves the things of this life.

Fourth, the sinful reasoning of the people is brought out in verse 10, where the Lord says, "Bring…" and then "I will… open you the windows of heaven." Offer, out of trust in me to supply your future needs, but offer *first!* In contrast, they reasoned this way: let God first give us plenty (open the windows) and then we will bring him the tithes and offerings. It was the "you first" mentality. "Thou, O God, must prove us, see if we will not indeed offer willingly when thou dost give us plenty to offer," rather than "proving" God, trusting him to supply future needs and rendering to him out of our present circumstances (Luke 21:2).

Valuable truths concerning our giving to God's church and to the poor, as well as our entire lives of stewardship are taught us.

God must be served first. The causes and needs of his kingdom come first. (1 Kings 17:13; Matt. 6:33).

We are taught proper stewardship. To rob is to take for oneself what belongs to another. We are taught by implication that all things belong to God and that he is to be served, not with some, but with all we have. (Ps. 24:1; 50:12).

The way of giving is the way of blessing. Greed, stinginess, and covetousness result in spiritual barrenness. We are not made poor by liberal giving to God's church and kingdom. Rather, we shall experience blessedness. (Mal. 3:10; 2 Cor. 9:8).

God calls the people to return (Mal. 3:7). See Jeremiah 31:18 for the relationship between God's grace and our turning from sin. One of the evidences of true spiritual repentance is seen in bringing in the tithes and offerings. Where grace has touched the heart, the hand is opened as well. (Luke 19:8; 2 Cor. 8:8).

The promise of God is twofold. First, "I will return unto you" (Mal. 3:7). That is, in the way of sincere stewardship we are given to enjoy the lovingkindness of God. Second, God will richly supply our earthly needs, often beyond our imaginations (v. 10).

In such a lesson as this we hear God speak, "Beware of covetousness, for a man's life does not consist in the abundance of things, but in being rich toward God" (Luke 12:15–21). How our carnal nature reveals itself when it comes to what we say is "ours," and we are called to render unto the Lord. May our study produce a "return," a seeking of God's glory first and a wise use of the earthly goods of our Master that have been entrusted to our stewardship (Matt. 25:14–30).

Study Questions and Activities

1. The relationship of the Christian to earthly things

   a. What is a steward (Ps. 50:7–23; Matt. 25:14–30)?

   b. Explain briefly the principles of stewardship.

c. What can we conclude from Romans 14:14, 20 and 1 Timothy 4:1–5 regarding material things?

d. Is it pious to be poor?

e. What is our fundamental calling toward earthly things (Rom. 14:6–9; 1 Cor. 10:23–33; Col. 3:23)?

2. The prophet exposes the evil of failing to bring in the tithes and offerings.

   a. What is the meaning of tithes? Consult a Bible dictionary or Bible encyclopedia.

   b. What do the following verses teach about tithing?

      1) Leviticus 27:30–32

      2) Numbers 18:21–32

      3) Deuteronomy 12:19

      4) Deuteronomy 14:22–29

c. What were the three steps in the process of tithing?

d. Offerings (see lesson 3)

   1) Does Malachi have in mind any particular offering
      that was being neglected or simply a general neglect
      of all things?

   2) The sin of not bringing in the tithes and offerings
      consisted in their robbing the Lord. To rob means
      "to defraud," "to hide," or "to cover." Explain the
      force of this.

   3) In what ways do we rob God (Heidelberg Catechism,
      Lord's Day 42)?

e. The sin of not bringing in the tithes and offerings con-
   sisted in covetousness. What do the following verses
   teach about covetousness?

   1) Luke 12:15–21

   2) Ephesians 5:5 and Colossians 3:5

   3) 2 Timothy 4:10

4) 1 Timothy 6:6–10

5) 1 Corinthians 12:31

f. What is the sin of covetousness? Find references in scripture and the creeds.

g. Why is covetousness idolatry?

h. In what areas of our lives does covetousness rear its ugly head?

i. The failure to bring the tithes and offerings revealed that Israel had not learned from the sins of their fathers (v. 7). Show that this sin was repeated in Israel's history (Ps. 78; Dan. 9; Ezek. 9).

j. Why is the history of God's gracious care for his people in past years so important for trust and contentment today?

3. The principles of giving

   a. Read 2 Corinthians 9 and list the important truths mentioned concerning the worship of giving.

b. Show and explain from Malachi 3:7–12 the following principles of giving:

   1) God first

   2) Stewardship

   3) The blessedness of giving

c. Make application of these principles to our lives today.

4. Repentance

   a. Examine the following passages in connection with verse 7:

      1) Jeremiah 18:11

      2) Jeremiah 31:18

      3) Lamentations 5:21

      4) Zechariah 1:3

      5) Canons of Dordt 3–4.16

b. What should have been Israel's response to God's call to return (Jer. 3:22)?

c. What are the graces God produces in a heart that turns from disobedience?

d. Why is our use of the material gifts of God a true indication of the attitude and state of our hearts toward God?

e. Therefore, what does the answer of the people indicate?

5. The promise of God

a. Will one ever become poor by reason of faithful, cheerful, and liberal giving to the causes of God and his kingdom (Ps. 31:19; 41:1–3; Prov. 3:9–10; 11:24–25; 19:17)? Why or why not?

b. Do we wait until we have enough of something before we give for the needs of God's church (Luke 21:1–4)?

c. What is the relationship between our giving and God's blessings, or God's provision for our future needs (1 Kings 17:8–16; 2 Kings 7:2, 19–20)?

d. What are the errors of the "health, wealth, and happiness gospel" so prevalent today (Prov. 30:7–9; Phil. 4:11; Heb. 13:5–6; James 4:2–3)?

"Bring ye all the tithes into the storehouse, that there may be meat in thine house, and prove to me now herewith, saith the Lord of hosts, if I will not open you the windows of heaven, and pour you out a blessing, that there shall not be room enough to receive it."—Malachi 3:10

"But rather seek ye the kingdom of God; and all these things shall be added unto you. Fear not, little flock; for it is your Father's good pleasure to give you the kingdom."—Luke 12:31–32

Recommended Reading

Arthur W. Pink, *Tithing*

Lesson 8

A God-Fearing Remnant in the Midst of a Hardened People

Malachi 3:13–18

Introduction

God will ever see to it that there is a people on earth who serve him even in the midst of the most hardened and callous spiritual apathy. As a jewel cast on a pile of coal, so in this section of Malachi we are shown a God-fearing remnant in the midst of the most blatant and blasphemous religious indifference. The words of Romans 11:5 are underscored in this lesson: "Even so then at this present time also there is a remnant according to the election of grace."

We are first given the full-blown and shameful truth of the spiritual coldness and deadness among many in Malachi's day (Mal. 3:13–15).

The unbelieving state of mind of many in Judah was expressed in their blasphemous talk against God. We have seen their back talk before (Mal. 1:7–8; 2:14, 17), but never to the horrible extent as confronted by Malachi now. Their words were "stout [strong]" against God.

Three elements are found in these words.

First, the people leveled two charges, or insults, against the justice of God. First, they claimed that they had served God and gained nothing by it (Mal. 3:14). Second, those who disobeyed God were not only unpunished but also blessed (v. 15). Their thinking was this: "Since we who serve Jehovah are not outwardly rewarded, and the proud heathen flourish in prosperity, we must conclude that God builds up the workers of iniquity and ignores those who render him service." It was the highest insult they could have spoken, and it brought God's severe judgment on them.

The second element is that the people presented to God an empty, outward service instead of true humility (v. 14). They claimed to have kept God's "ordinance [charge]" and to have walked "mournfully [walked in black]." But it was all false pretense. They were swollen with false confidence, for they were pretending to be low before God, when in reality they were "stout"! Though they claimed to be modest and submissive, in reality they were swelled with presumption as they daringly and furiously spoke evil of God. Calvin offers the following perceptive comments on their true state:

> They thought they worshipped God perfectly; and this was their false principle; for hypocrites ever lay claim to complete holiness, and cannot bear to confess their own evils; even when their conscience goads them, they deceive themselves with vain flatteries, and always endeavor to draw over them some veil that their disgrace may not appear before men.

The third element in the words of the people is that when the prophet reproved them they were defiant (v. 13). Their hardness had reached a point where they could not be checked. To the charge that they had spoken against God they responded that they had been falsely accused. They were conscious of no wrong.

Yet, we must not conclude that the words of Malachi produced no fruit to God's glory. A remnant, a faithful element, was brought under conviction as they listened to the prophet, and they turned to God and to one another in repentance (vv. 16–17).

Let us note from verse 16 the following elements in them.

First, they feared the Lord. This was their prominent characteristic, as it is mentioned twice in verse 16. The fear of God is loving reverence for God. The essential elements of the fear of God are a correct conception of the character of God, a pervasive sense of the presence of God, and a constant awareness of our obligations to God.

Second, they thought upon God's name. This must be understood in the sense of hallowed meditation on the character of God as revealed in his names (Ps. 20).

Third, they spoke among themselves. This means that an evidence of true repentance was seen in their relations with others. Those who fear the Lord and are brought to humble repentance must also unite themselves to one another "so that with one consent they may return to the way [from which] they had departed, yea, that they may return to God whom they had forsaken" (Calvin).

Fourth, a book of remembrance was written. This was a sign of the truth that they had been turned to God and had then vowed to devote themselves to him. It would also serve as a reminder in the days to come and thus be an encouragement to the faithful.

How marvelous is the promise of God spoken to a repentant, God-fearing, recommitted remnant (v. 17)! The Lord had blessed the labor of Malachi and made it profitable to some, even though we are not told their number.

The promise spoken to the remnant is rich (v. 17). God owns them as his own (Isa. 43:1–7). The word "jewels" is literally "my possession" or "treasure" (Ex. 19:5). He promises to spare them from the judgments that must fall on the impenitent, and to do this in the compassion and fervor that a father would show to his son. He speaks of a future day when he shall make up his final possession by drawing out of all ages and nations, including these repentant members of Judah, and making them into one treasure of the Lord (Eph. 1:10).

The lesson concludes with the announcement that there shall also come the time when the difference will be clearly shown between the righteous and the wicked (Mal. 3:18). In that day (Mal. 4:1) every man will appear in his true colors, and the righteous judgments of God will be perfectly seen (Rom. 2:5–16). Malachi then returns (v. 18) to the charges the hardened members of Judah had brought against the Lord; and he answers them, "God will at length rise to judgment, and then all shall know that the deeds of men do not go unnoticed by him and that wickedness shall not go unpunished."

May God use our study to work in us the same blessed fruit mentioned in Malachi 3:16–17. What can compare with God's promise "they shall be mine"?

Study Questions and Activities

1. The hardened state of many in Judah formed the background (blackground?) to the wonderful fruit of the repentance of the remnant. We will want to understand the carnal mentality behind their back talk to God, how it developed, and how it is a temptation to us as well. Compare the responses to the prophet's indictments recorded in this prophecy, jotting down a note on each one.

   a. Malachi 1:6

   b. Malachi 1:12

   c. Malachi 1:13

   d. Malachi 2:14

   e. Malachi 2:17

   f. Malachi 3:7

   g. Malachi 3:8

   h. Malachi 3:13–15

1) What were the common ingredients in these responses?

2) What attitude came across?

3) Is there a discernable progression in these responses?

4) How are these responses to God's reproofs evident today?

5) How are these responses to God's reproofs evident in our lives?

6) Look up Proverbs 6:20–23 and 2 Timothy 3:16–17 and discuss this statement: If we cannot submit to the reproofs of scripture and see how we must be warned, the scriptures are of no profit to us.

2. The two criticisms of God's justice (vv. 14–15)

   a. "It is vain to serve God."

      1) Examine Psalm 73:13 and Matthew 19:27 and compare them to Israel's criticism.

2) What was the reasoning behind their criticism, or what was their root thinking that led them to say that it was vain to serve God?

3) In what ways can we guard against this sin?

b. "And now we call the proud happy."

   1) What did they mean by this criticism (Ps. 73:3)?

   2) How could the people of that day come to that conclusion?

   3) Compare the following verses. What do they teach about this?

      (a) Ecclesiastes 8:11–13

      (b) Ecclesiastes 9:1–2

      (c) Romans 2:6–16

   4) Does God postpone judgment (Heidelberg Catechism, Lord's Day 4, Q&A 10; Mal. 3:18)?

3. The people claimed that they had "kept God's ordinance, and...walked mournfully before God."

    a. Was this true? Why or why not?

    b. Look up Isaiah 58:1–7 and Micah 6:6–8.

        1) What are the symptoms of a pretend humility and service of God?

        2) What are the elements of true lowliness before God?

4. Verses 16–17 are certainly very rich and precious, as they reveal the response of the God-fearing to the message of God's prophet and the tenderness of their hearts to be pricked and thus to repent and return to God.

    a. What accounted for their sincere repentance (1 Kings 19:10–18; Rom. 11:3–6)?

    b. What is the "fear of God"? Consult a Bible concordance and select three or four passages that express the heart of fearing God.

        1) Why are the following three elements necessary for the fear of God?

           (a) Right conceptions of God

(b) A pervading sense of God's power

(c) A heartfelt recognition of one's obligations to God

2) Is the fear of God the most basic and distinguishing mark of a Christian? Why or why not? Prove from scripture.

3) How is the fear of God nurtured in ourselves?

4) How is the fear of God nurtured in our children?

c. "They that feared the LORD spake often one to another."

1) Look up the following passages. How do they teach that repentance before God and reconciliation with one another are inseparable?

(a) Matthew 18:21–35

(b) 2 Corinthians 7:9–11 (especially v. 11)

(c) 1 John 4: 20– 21

2) Why are repentance and reconciliation inseparable?

d. What is the significance of the "book of remembrance" that was written?

5. God's comforting promise to a truly humbled and repentant people (v. 17)

a. What is the significance of God's making us his possession ("jewels") (Ex. 19:5; Ps. 135:4)?

b. What is meant by God's promise to "spare them"?

c. In what day will God make up his possession (Matt. 25:31–33; Eph. 1:10)?

d. Read Isaiah 43:1–6.

1) What comfort do you derive from God's promise: "Thou art mine...I will be with thee" (vv. 1–2)?

2) How ought this to be held before our minds in our daily lives?

"Then they that feared the Lord spake often one to another: and the Lord hearkened, and heard it, and a book of remembrance was written before him for them that feared the Lord, and that thought upon his name. And they shall be mine, saith the Lord of hosts, in that day when I make up my jewels; and I will spare them, as a man spareth his own son that serveth him."—Malachi 3:16–17

"Even so then at this present time also there is a remnant according to the election of grace. And if by grace, then it is no more of works: otherwise grace is no more grace. But if it be of works, then it is no more grace: otherwise work is no more work."—Romans 11:5–6

Lesson 9

Behold, the Day Comes

Malachi 4

Introduction

Chapter 4 of Malachi's prophecy flows naturally from the thoughts of the last part of chapter 3. Chapter 3:17–18 speaks of that day when God would at last make up his church, in which the remnant of Malachi's day would be included. Malachi also says that the day would be one of vindication of God's righteous judgments when the difference between the righteous and wicked would be clearly shown. Now the prophet declares the *certainty* of the day: "behold, the day cometh." Malachi also unfolds the *events* of that day: judgment for all who do wickedly and salvation for all who fear God's name.

It should impress us that this is a very significant chapter. Not only is it the conclusion of Malachi's prophecy, but it is also the end of the Old Testament. The next word from God would be when the angel Gabriel is sent to Zacharias in the temple. We could not think of a more fitting and sober conclusion to both Malachi's prophecy and the Old Testament. The certainty of Christ's coming is announced, the warning of final judgment, the announcement of the arrival of Elijah to prepare God's people for that day, and the encouragement on account of the great good that will belong to God's people — all these are found in this chapter.

Dividing the thoughts of chapter 4, we see that the day Malachi foretells as surely coming will be, first, a day of *judgment*. The prophet describes the day as "the great and dreadful day of the LORD" (v. 5). Further, it will be the day of destruction and fiery indignation of God against the wicked that will leave them nothing (v. 1). And finally, it will be the day when Jehovah will smite the earth with a curse. The prophet sees plainly ahead to the last day ushered in by the appearing of Christ, resulting in the final judgment and damnation of the wicked.

The second thought of the chapter is *renewal*. Before that day comes (and remember Malachi sees the day of the Lord as one whole: Christ's birth and his second coming for judgment), Elijah will come. His work will be to turn the hearts of God's people. Specifically, there will be a renewal of the family and of the covenant, as the hearts of the fathers will be turned to their children and the hearts of the children will be turned to their fathers. Elijah's ministry will result in a people made ready for the day of Christ's return. Thus the prophet calls us to remember the "law of Moses my servant" (v. 4).

The third thought of the chapter is *salvation*. That which will bring judgment to the wicked world at the same time will bring salvation to those who fear the Lord. Indeed, the purpose for the day is the glory of God seen in the salvation of his church. That salvation is beautifully described. Christ will come as the Sun of righteousness to give light and healing. The elect will share in his victory and tread down the wicked (v. 2; 1 Cor. 6:2; Heidelberg Catechism, Lord's Day 12, Q&A 32). Matthew Henry says so well:

> The great and terrible day of the Lord, like the pillar of cloud and fire, shall have a dark side turned towards the Egyptians that fight against God, and a bright side towards the faithful Israelites that follow him.

We are taught to look forward to that day, to keep ourselves unspotted from the world as we wait, and to be faithful in our homes until he appears in power and great glory (2 Thess. 1:7–10).

Study Questions and Activities

1. The day of the Lord: judgment

   a. From verses 1, 5–6 write down what Malachi says about the day of the Lord.

b. What will be the overall impression left upon the wicked?

c. Look up the following passages. What do they teach about the day of the Lord?

1) Isaiah 34:1–10

2) Revelation 6:12–17

3) 2 Thessalonians 1:7–10

4) 2 Peter 3:7–14

d. Find other scriptural passages that speak of the day of the Lord.

e. What will happen to the physical creation at the day of the Lord?

f. What is the idea of "fire" in scripture?

g. What is implied in the burning up of the earth and the wicked?

h. Will they be annihilated?

i. Judgment will come upon "the proud and all that do wickedly." From this prophecy explain who is meant by the "proud" and by those who "do wickedly."

j. Put this in today's terms.

2. The day of the Lord: renewal

   a. Verse 5 says that Elijah will be sent before the day of the Lord comes.

   b. Who is Elijah (Matt. 11:13–14; 17:10–13; Mark 9:12; Luke 1:15–17; 16:16)?

   c. What are the similarities between Elijah and John the Baptist?

   d. Give illustrations from their lives of their similarities.

   e. Is the ministry of Elijah (John the Baptist) finished, or is it still present?

f. If Elijah's ministry is still present, where is it present?

g. Explain and prove your answers above from the Bible.

h. The result of the sending of Elijah the prophet (v. 6)

1) When Gabriel quotes this passage to Zacharias, he changes part of it (Mal 4:6; Luke 1:17).

   (a) What does he change?

   (b) What is the significance of this change?

2) What does it mean that the hearts of the fathers will be turned to their children (Isa. 38:19; Eph. 6:4; Col. 3:21)?

3) What does it mean that the hearts of children will be turned to their fathers (Luke 2:51; Eph. 6:1–3; Col. 3:20)?

4) The result of the faithful ministry performed in the spirit of Elijah is found first and primarily in the home and parent-child relationship. We may call it a covenantal renewal. Give some of the traits of a home where the hearts of parents are turned to their children, and children to their parents.

5) How are these traits cultivated or nurtured?

3. The day of the Lord: salvation

   a. Verse 2 is one of the great Old Testament prophecies of our Lord and the salvation he brings.

      1) What does it mean that he is the "Sun of righteousness?"

      2) Explain the "healing in his wings."

   b. The effect of his coming upon us is that "ye shall go forth, and grow up as calves of the stall." A very expressive and beautiful figure is used of releasing to the field calves that have been tied up all winter.

      1) Explain what that verse and figure mean.

      2) What spiritual emotions are worked in us at the coming of Christ?

   c. Verse 3 shows that we will share in the victory of Christ over the wicked (1 Cor. 6:1–2).

      1) Why is this important?

      2) How is this encouragement to us?

d. Malachi sees the day of the Lord as one, including his birth and return. What does this teach us?

e. What will characterize the church (us) as we await the coming of Christ (v. 4)?

"But unto you that fear my name shall the Sun of righteousness arise with healing in his wings; and ye shall go forth, and grow up as calves of the stall. Behold, I will send you Elijah the prophet before the coming of the great and dreadful day of the LORD: And he shall turn the heart of the fathers to the children, and the heart of the children to their fathers, lest I come and smite the earth with a curse."—Malachi 4:2, 5–6).